GROWING UP

Having an Eye Test

Vic Parker

www.raintreepublishers.co.uk
Visit our website to find out
more information about
Raintree books.

To order:
☎ Phone 0845 6044371
🖨 Fax +44 (0) 1865 312263
✉ Email myorders@raintreepublishers.co.uk

Customers from outside the UK please telephone +44 1865 312262

Raintree is an imprint of Capstone Global Library
Limited, a company incorporated in England and Wales
having its registered office at 7 Pilgrim Street, London,
EC4V 6LB – Registered company number: 6695582

Edited by Dan Nunn, Rebecca Rissman, and Sian Smith
Designed by Joanna Hinton-Malivoire
Picture research by Elizabeth Alexander
Originated by Capstone Global Library Ltd
Printed and bound in China by Leo Paper
Products Ltd

ISBN 978 1 406 22047 6 (hardback)
15 14 13 12 11
10 9 8 7 6 5 4 3 2 1

British Library Cataloguing in Publication Data
Parker, Victoria.
   Having an eye test. – (Growing up)
   1. Vision–Testing–Pictorial works–Juvenile
literature. 2. Opticianry–Pictorial works–Juvenile
literature.
   I. Title II. Series

617.7'52-dc22

Acknowledgements
We would like to thank the following for permission
to reproduce photographs: Alamy pp. 10 (© amana
images inc.), 14, 16, 23 glossary expert (© Image
Source), 18 (© Sally and Richard Greenhill); Birmingham
and Midland Eye Centre p. 12; Corbis pp. 5 (© Bernd
Vogel), 17 (© JLP/Jose L. Pelaez), 21 (© Pauline St.
Denis); Getty Images p. 8 (altrendo images/Stockbyte);
iStockphoto pp. 4 (© Rob Friedman), 11 (© Izabela
Habur); Photolibrary pp. 6 (Leah Warkentin/Design
Pics Inc), 9, 23 glossary optician (UpperCut Images);
Science Photo Library pp. 20, 23 glossary eye drops
(David Hay Jones), 19, 23 glossary eye patch (Mark
Clarke); Shutterstock pp. 7 (© Elena Elisseeva), 13, 23
glossary lenses (© GWImages), 15 (© lightpoet).

Front cover photograph of a boy looking at eye
examination equipment reproduced with permission of
Alamy (© Blend Images). Back cover photographs of
an optician reproduced with permission of iStockphoto
(© Izabela Habur), and lenses reproduced with
permission of Shutterstock (© GWImages).

We would like to thank Rosie Auld for her invaluable
help and support in the preparation of this book.

Every effort has been made to contact copyright
holders of material reproduced in this book. Any
omissions will be rectified in subsequent printings if
notice is given to the publisher.

Contents

Some words are shown in bold, **like this**.
You can find them in the glossary on page 23.

What is an eye test?

You see things with your eyes.

An eye test is a check to see that both your eyes are working properly.

An eye test will make sure you can see things that are close up.

It will also make sure you can see things that are far away.

Why might I have an eye test?

You might have an eye test because you have reached a certain age.

Most children have eye tests during their first year at school.

Sometimes your teacher, parent, or doctor might think you have a problem with your sight.

You may have an eye test then, too.

Where will it happen?

Some eye tests are done at school.

The eye test might happen in the school nurse's room or in an empty classroom.

Many people have their eyes tested
in a shop called an **optician's**.

You can buy glasses at an optician's,
too.

Who will I meet?

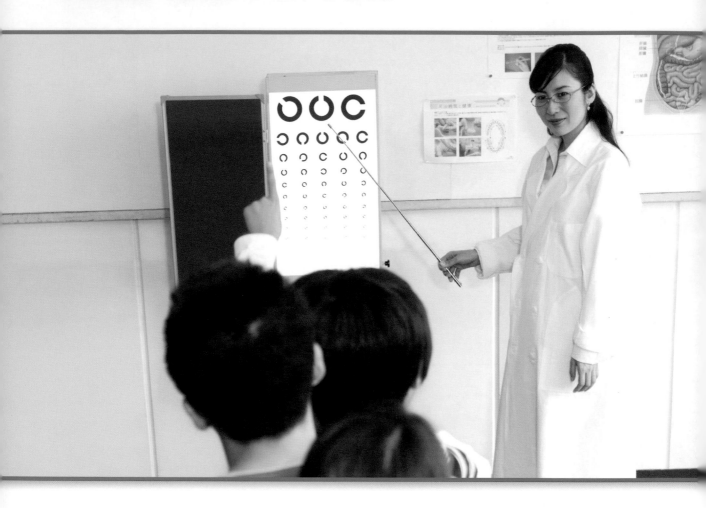

Sometimes an eye **expert** will come in to school to do eye tests.

Sometimes eye tests at school are done by the school nurse.

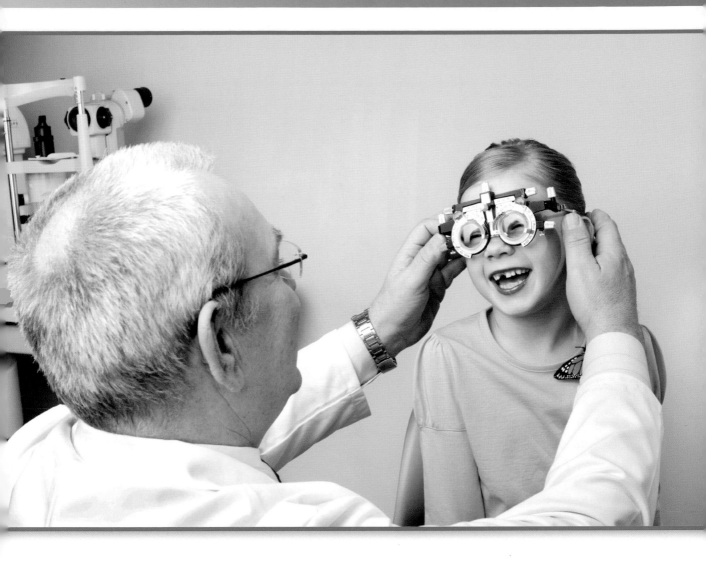

If you go to an **optician's** shop, your eye test will be done by an **optician**.

Opticians are eye experts too.

What will I have to do?

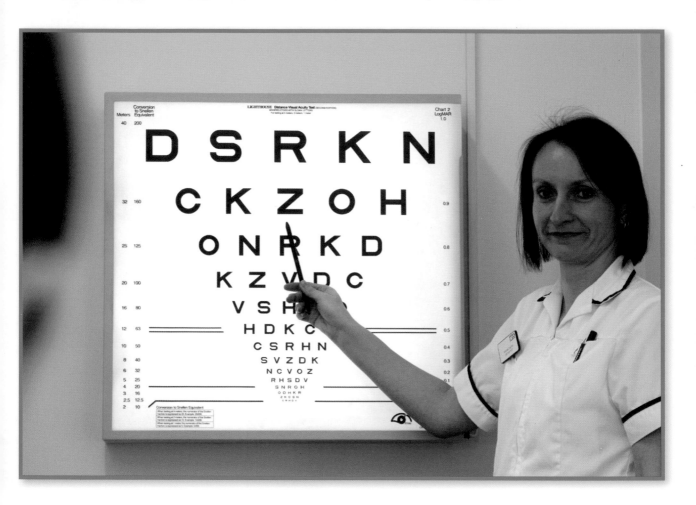

With one eye covered, you will look at a chart with letters on it and say what you can see.

Then you will do it again with the other eye covered.

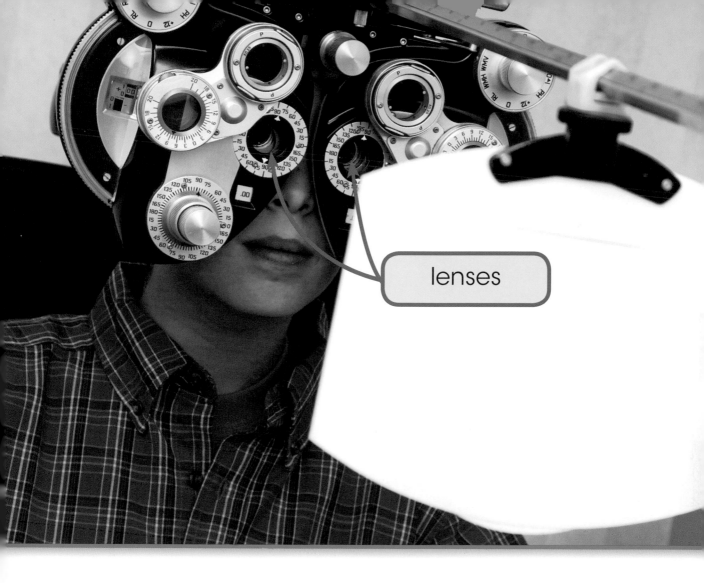

lenses

You may have to look at a picture through some special equipment.

The eye **expert** will change **lenses** in the equipment and ask you if the picture is clearer or more blurry.

What other equipment might I see?

You may see a small torch used to shine a bright light at your eye.

You may also see a big machine that you have to sit at.

The eye **expert** uses both of these to look inside your eyes.

This helps him or her find out if you need to wear glasses.

Will I need to wear glasses?

If an eye test shows that you have a problem, you might need to wear glasses.

There are lots of frames to choose from.

Glasses may help you see things close up or far away.

They can also help if one eye doesn't see as well as the other one.

What other help may I have for my sight?

If you need more help with your sight, then sometimes other tests are done.

You may go to a hospital to have these tests.

Some people find that one eye is weaker
than the other.

Sometimes wearing an **eye patch** for a
while can help to make it stronger.

Will the eye test hurt?

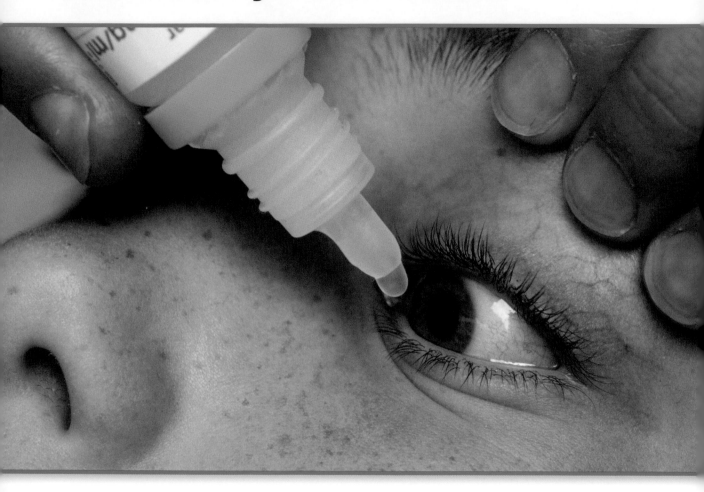

Some parts of your eye test may be uncomfortable. For example, if you need **eye drops,** it can feel odd.

But nothing during an eye test will hurt.

It is natural to feel a little nervous about your eye test.

But everything the eye **expert** does is to help you.

Tips to keep your eyes healthy

Do:

- ✓ eat plenty of fruit and vegetables
- ✓ wear sunglasses in bright light
- ✓ rinse your eyes with water if you get dirt or dust in them.

Don't:

- ✗ stick things into your eyes
- ✗ sit too close or for too long at the computer or TV
- ✗ rub your eyes.

Picture glossary

expert someone who knows a lot about something and has special skills in that area

eye drops special medicine for your eyes

eye patch plaster or piece of cloth worn over one eye

lenses see-through shapes that you can look through to help you see things either close up or far away

optician someone who tests your eyesight. The shop where an optician works is called an "optician's".

Find out more

Books

Healthy Eyes and Ears (Look After Yourself), Angela Royston (Heinemann Library, 2006)

Optician (People Who Help Us), Deborah Chancellor (Franklin Watts, 2007)

Sight (The Senses), Mandy Suhr (Wayland, 2007)

Websites

Learn more about eyesight and other parts of your body at: **kidshealth.org/kid/**

Discover more about your amazing eyes at: **www.childrenfirst.nhs.uk**

Index